ROBERT CAVELIER
DE LA SALLE

ROBERT CAVELIER
DE LA SALLE
W. J. Jacobs

A Visual Biography

*Illustrated with authentic prints,
documents, and maps*

Franklin Watts, Inc. / New York / 1975

Historical consultant,
Professor Frederick Kershner, Jr.,
Teachers College, Columbia University

Library of Congress Cataloging in Publication Data

Jacobs, William Jay.
    Robert Cavelier de La Salle.

    (A Visual biography)
    Bibliography: p.
    Includes index.
    SUMMARY: A brief biography of the seven-
teenth-century French explorer who traveled the
entire length of the Mississippi and took possession of all its surrounding territory for France.
    1. La Salle, Robert Cavelier, sieur de, 1643–
1687—Juvenile literature.   [1. La Salle, Robert
Cavelier, sieur de, 1643–1687.   2. Explorers]
I. Title.
F1030.5.J33   970′.02′0924 [B] [92]
ISBN 0–531–02843–7   75–8598

For the librarians of the
Free Public Library
Rutherford, New Jersey.
With appreciation.

A Note on the Illustrations

Many of the illustrations in this book are from Father Louis Hennepin's various volumes, written and published after his personal association with La Salle. The engravings of this period seem to combine fact and fantasy and present an interesting comment on the New World. There are reproductions of several documents and maps belonging to La Salle and to his contemporaries.

In addition, the original maps drawn especially for this book by William K. Plummer are marked WKP.

Illustration credits

Archives Nationales du Québec,
Collection Initiale: pp. vi, 5, 26 (top)

Public Archives of Canada: pp. 7, 8,
14 (top and bottom), 21 (top and bottom),
26 (bottom), 37 (top), 40 (bottom), 45, 52

Library of Congress: pp. 37 (bottom),
46 (top and bottom), 49

Royal Ontario Museum, Toronto: pp. 37 (center), 50

New York Public Library,
Picture Collection: p. 40 (top)

Corporation of the City of Kingston, Ontario: p. 18

Original maps by William K. Plummer
Photo research by Selma Hamdan
Cover design by Rafael Hernandez

René-Robert Cavelier, Sieur de La Salle

It was April 9, 1682. On that date explorer René-Robert Cavelier, Sieur de La Salle, proudly implanted the flag of France alongside a wooden cross at the mouth of the mighty Mississippi River. It was his moment of triumph, the high point of his career.

With that simple ceremony La Salle laid claim for France, in the name of King Louis XIV, to all of the vast territory whose rivers flowed into "the father of waters." The land he claimed—the fabulous "Louisiana"—comprised an area many times the size of the French homeland. And until 1803, when Napoleon Bonaparte sold it to Thomas Jefferson in history's most incredible real estate deal, Louisiana was to be the foundation of France's continuing dream of a great colonial empire in the New World.

La Salle—unlike Cortes, Pizarro, and even some of the early French and English explorers—was no greedy seeker after gold. He gave up a promising fur-trading business in Montreal and borrowed money at outrageous rates of interest to finance his daring expeditions. Glory, for its own sake, held little appeal for him; although a fine writer, he never troubled to publicize his exploits. Nor was he especially interested in converting the Indians to Christianity.

For La Salle the attraction of exploring a wilderness continent lay in great enterprises: the discovery of a water route to China through the North American continent; the conquest of

Mexico from Spain; the total triumph of France over all rival nations. For him, nothing less than a grand adventure would do, an adventure that would be a supreme test of his determination, his energy—his will.

To the poet Longfellow, La Salle's achievement could be summed up as "the life of a man of genius, resisting all temptations, laying aside all fears, heedless of all warnings, and pressing right on to accomplish his purpose."

That La Salle's goals of conquest (like those of Alexander the Great) were boundless—without limits—only serves to make him a more intriguing personality. His successes were enormous. He and his party were among the first Europeans to penetrate deeply into the interior of the continent. He descended the Mississippi to the Gulf of Mexico, may have been the first white man to see the Ohio, and explored the shores of the Great Lakes. If, in the end, he failed to realize his romantic dreams, it does not diminish the grandeur of his deeds.

The saga of La Salle is that of a man risking greatly, casting the dice in quest of what perhaps even he himself knew was an impossible goal. Yet relentlessly he persisted, brushing aside all thought of consequences to himself and his men. For La Salle, the story ended unhappily. Yet the life he lived, driven, unbending, single-minded, provides a fascinating chapter in the history of adventure.

THE LURE
OF CANADA

René-Robert Cavelier enjoyed a fortunate childhood. Intelligent and strong, he was the second son of a prosperous merchant of Rouen, France. From the time of his birth in November, 1643, he profited from all the advantages that came with wealth and his family's favored social position. The title "Sieur de La Salle," by which he is known to history, was drawn from the name of the Caveliers' country estate; it was a common practice among wealthy Frenchmen to give family members such titles. In addition to an older brother, Robert also had a younger brother and a sister.

As a boy La Salle was a devoted Catholic. He responded eagerly to his father's desire that he study to become a priest. Hoping to serve the Church as an overseas missionary, he joined the Jesuit Order. The Jesuits, probably the most militant of Catholic religious orders, followed a rigorous, demanding plan of education. They sharpened La Salle's quick mind, training him to state an argument clearly and convincingly and to write with precision.

But the Jesuits were never able to instill in young La Salle a spirit of obedience. Independent, determined to issue commands of his own, he was unwilling merely to obey others. Before long he began to develop a distaste for the Jesuits. At the age of twenty-two, when his father died, he left the order. According to French law, however, a person joining a religious community gave up his right to inherit family wealth. La Salle was therefore forced to live on an allowance, dependent on the goodwill of his relatives. Always proud, he found such a situation intolerable.

He had little desire to follow in his father's footsteps as a merchant in Rouen. What did appeal to him was travel and adventure. His older brother, Jean Cavelier, was already a priest in Canada, and the ambitious Robert calculated that he might have a chance in the New World to carve out an exciting and successful life of his own.

In the spring of 1666, not yet twenty-three years old, he sailed for Canada.

Arriving at Montreal, he was welcomed with enthusiasm. Jean Cavelier had recommended his younger brother as a man of energy and determination. Such pioneers were desperately needed in New France, as Canada was known at that time. The priests of Jean's religious community, the Order of Saint Sulpice, provided young René-Robert Cavelier, Sieur de La Salle, with a sizable land grant on the western edge of Montreal. He in turn agreed to recruit settlers from France to live on the land.

La Salle marked out the boundaries of a village which he called Saint Sulpice, although it was sometimes referred to as "La Chine," since it was close to the so-called China Rapids on the Saint Lawrence River. Each settler was given about one third of an acre inside the fortified village and forty acres outside the palisaded enclosure. For a small annual fee the settlers were also permitted to share in common grazing land for their livestock.

Patiently La Salle began to clear the land he had set aside for his own use. His land holdings were strategically located up the Saint Lawrence from Montreal, giving him an excellent position for the fur trade with the Indians. If he had chosen to do so, he

Montreal, as it appeared about 1642

could have lived the rest of his life in wealth and relative comfort. After only two years as a fur trader and farmer he had already become prosperous.

But La Salle was restless and ambitious. Two Seneca Indians visiting his home over the winter told him of a great river, far away, that flowed into the sea. To the dreamer La Salle, the story could mean only one thing—the long-sought "passage to India," a way through the North American continent to the Pacific Ocean. Actually the Indians spoke of two rivers: the *Ohio*, or "Beautiful Water," and the "Missi-Sepe, or "Big Water." Either or both, thought La Salle, might lead to the "Vermilion Sea," or Gulf of California, beyond which lay the Orient.

Afire with enthusiasm but without much money, La Salle journeyed to Quebec to ask permission for an expedition. He was sure that if there really was a connecting link to the ocean, he could find it. The prize would be fame equal to that of Christopher Columbus.

Governor de Courcelle gave his permission but no financial aid. La Salle was able, however, to persuade the Abbé de Queylus of the Sulpicians to buy back most of the land that the order had originally granted him for nothing—paying about one thousand livres (equivalent today to about six thousand dollars) for the improvements he had made. Queylus was reluctant to see La Salle leave, considering him a valuable asset to Montreal. The priest refused to buy back all of the land grant and even conferred on the young would-be explorer a noble title, giving him the rights of a feudal lord over the remaining land. But it was no use. La

*The document of sale of
La Salle's land at
La Chine to the Sulpicians,
January 9, 1669*

aud. Montreal, L'an 1769 Soixante et
Neuf, Le Neufieme jour de Janvier après midy
Scavoir pour led. Sieur acceptant en cas leur
aud. lieu, et pour led. Sieur Coddaue ch la maison,
ou Il est presentement demourant, presens Sieurs
Galiniere en faveur d'aller demoniers q
remuaux q soulz seignez avec Ledit Sieur de Coddaue,
acceptant q Galiniere, ↑ Galiniere
↑ premiere aud. Sieur Coddaue, pour pot de lui,
Lamoitier d'Eng pore brack, qui luy Sera delivré par
Ledit Sieur galiniere, approuvé cedant en Inte et ligne
et un mot en rature. R. de La Salle
                    Labbe...
                    Bassck

Aujourd'huy Est Comparu pardevant Le Nottaire
Susditt et presens les tesmoings desnommez et soubz nommés
René Cauelier Sieur de la Salle, Coddaue desnommé au
courbart de Cession Sur Escrit, Lequel a Recconu et
confessé, Avoir pardez ey devant en recem de M.
Dominique Galinie Prestre et Occonomé de la Maison
des Messieurs Les Ecclesiastiques dolad. Isle q seignur
Dlle La Somme de quatre une Cinox Cinquante
d'bonne Marchandise en Linois, Le L...M Mosieur
predenommé de M Mathieu Ramuye Seg ordible L
Ecclesiastique q Occonome Dleur Maison, La Somme
de Six Cent Linois, en Marchandise, q comprise La
Some de Deux Cent linove que led. Sr Ramuye a
payé en Sieur Jean Milon Cuillandier q les lieux
a Lacquict dud. Sieur de la salle, q la somme de
Cem Soixant q Six linove Six linoz Solz, que led.
Sieur Ramuye a gavellemme payé au Nommé Rene
Culaire de L'eueille aussy Lacq dud lieu, q à Lacquict
dud Sieur de la salle, Rumb et Less. A douz Somme
de quatre Cem linove q Six Cem linove a Celle de M.Linove
que ... de Seuchaire St Sulpice du Fauxbourg St Germain, des prez

Preces Illinicae.

pro signo crucis.

Nasingachiro dieu sekvississiane,
sevssiane minava, pekisita minava
sitelimanetseiane. neve echino-
gatokitche.

Acte de foi
de la presence de Dieu.

Kitchiakimamamanetaviane
kitaramitsve, Tchefi minsi
tekakvapiani, sahi cheskvigi
tekakvapiva ireximivani; Tcheki

kiku nundamáni, Tcheki kiku
minava pekunansivani, neve kata
nunghi nundaluani Tcheki. keku
tanemissunghi iveveaniva, tane

Salle had made up his mind. He sold the rest of his holdings—, along with his new title—to an ironworker.

With the money from the sale of his estate he outfitted four canoes and hired fourteen men to accompany him. At the request of Governor de Courcelle he was joined by another party led by a Sulpician priest, François Dollier de Casson. The Sulpicians hoped to rival the Jesuits in making conversions among the Indians. Dollier had just returned from a journey among the Nipissings, a tribe living between Lake Huron and Lake Ontario.

Courageous, exceptionally strong, and a soldier in his youth, Dollier had practical experience with the problems of exploring the wilderness. And although La Salle had looked forward to undisputed leadership of the expedition, he welcomed the priest into his planning. The Sulpicians equipped three canoes for the journey.

On July 6, 1669, the combined parties, consisting of seven canoes and twenty-four men, set out from La Chine. Two canoes, bearing Seneca Indian guides, traveled at the head of the column.

The first page of a book of prayers in the language of the Illinois Indians, made about 1668 by the Jesuit Father Allouez

EASTERN CANADA
MID-1600s

NOUVELLE-FRANCE

Lake Huron

Lake

Niagara Portage

Lake Erie

Quebec •

Three Rivers •

Montreal •

La Chine
Rapids •

Fort
Frontenac •

Ontario

St. Lawrence River

ATLANTIC OCEAN

WKP.

EARLY
EXPLORATIONS

Exploring was a new experience for almost all the Frenchmen in the group. The food was strange—mostly boiled Indian corn seasoned with fish; all of the supplies and canoes had to be portaged (carried) between rivers and streams; the travelers were exposed to the elements without shelter. As one Sulpician priest, Father Galinée, described the journey:

> *This sort of life seemed so strange to us, that we all felt the effects of it; and, before we were a hundred leagues from Montreal, not one of us was free from some malady or another.*

The Sulpicians urged a rest at a mission outpost maintained by their order on the north shore of Lake Ontario. But La Salle, preferring not to lose any days of good summer weather, insisted on pressing on.

One month after leaving La Chine the explorers encountered a party of Seneca Indians. The Senecas, like all the tribes of the Iroquois Confederacy, had been hostile to the French since the French explorer Champlain joined the Hurons and Algonquins in warring against them. But La Salle, Galinée, and eight other Frenchmen accepted the Indians' invitation to visit the village; the others were left behind to guard the canoes.

The white men were treated as honored guests. They feasted on dog meat and were given many gifts. As a special entertainment, the Senecas brought in a captured warrior from a neighboring tribe. They bound him to a stake and, for six hours, slowly tortured him. Finally turning him loose, they proceeded to stone him to death. Then they ripped his body apart and devoured him piece by piece.

Some of the Indians proposed making La Salle and his countrymen their next dinners. But the elders of the tribe refused. Sickened by what they had seen and fearful of what lay ahead—which is probably the effect the Senecas hoped to achieve—the Frenchmen left as soon as they could.

Skirting close enough to Niagara Falls to hear the roar of its cascading waters, La Salle and his men stopped at an Indian village. There they found a captive warrior who promised to guide them to the Ohio River. Surprisingly, there were also two other Frenchmen in the village. One was the former Jesuit priest turned fur trader and explorer, Louis Jolliet.

Jolliet had been trying unsuccessfully to locate copper deposits along the shores of Lake Superior. He told the Sulpician priests about the Potawatomi Indians he had met, savages, said Jolliet, who were in dire need of conversion to Christianity. The Sulpicians, enthusiastic, decided to continue into the upper Great Lakes area to try their hand at working with the Indian tribes.

La Salle argued strongly against their decision but could not sway them. Determined to push on to his goal—the Ohio and Mississippi river valleys—he claimed to be ill from a fever and unable to accompany the priests on their mission. This story, he reasoned, would allow him to press forward without offending the devout Sulpicians, whom he admired.

The parting of the two groups was friendly, marked by a mass conducted in the woods by Father Dollier. The Sulpicians set off to the northwest, La Salle and his followers to the south.

The Sulpicians encountered one difficulty after another on their journey. Finally, following a storm one night on Lake Erie, they landed exhausted on a beach, too tired even to move their baggage. By morning most of it, including the sacred objects for their altar, had been swept away. Having failed to convert even a single Indian, the missionaries returned to Montreal. Most of the city's population placed the blame on La Salle for abandoning them.

Meanwhile, La Salle was in considerable difficulty. Several of his men deserted him, frightened by stories told by the Senecas about dangers in the Ohio River valley. Some of the deserters returned to Montreal; others took refuge from the snows and cold of winter among Dutch and English colonists.

What La Salle did from 1669 to early 1673 is not clear. Some accounts, including that of the great American historian Francis Parkman, say that during those years La Salle continued on with just a few followers and successfully explored the Ohio and Illinois river valleys. Whether, in fact, he actually reached the Ohio is disputed by recent writers. Nevertheless, it was on the basis of La Salle's supposed discoveries that the French later built Fort Duquesne (Pittsburgh) at the source of the Ohio River and,

Above, the frontispiece from Historiae canadensis, *published in Paris in 1664, depicting the martyrdom of the early Jesuit missionaries. Below, Niagara Falls, from Father Hennepin's* A New Discovery of a Vast Country in America.

without protest from Great Britain, laid claim to the entire Ohio valley.

Although the path of La Salle's wanderings is not known, it is certain that he stayed in the wilderness. His time was spent hunting, fishing, living with the Indians and learning their languages, learning the skills of survival that would later contribute to his success.

Legal records reveal that by late December, 1672, he had returned to Montreal at least once; it is also possible that he had returned once before, in August, 1671. His activities aroused little comment. He had not discovered his "passage to India," and his continued interest in the project exposed him to ridicule. Moreover, as many chose to remember, he had abandoned the Sulpician priests far from civilization in order to pursue his own private goals. His popularity was at low ebb.

But better times were ahead for La Salle. In 1672 a new governor had been appointed for New France—the Count de Frontenac.

FRONTENAC
AND LA SALLE

Like La Salle, the Count de Frontenac was ambitious. He hoped to build a fort on the shores of Lake Ontario to keep the Indians in check and to control the fur trade. This would help make New France safer from Indian attacks; it would also make those few men who held a monopoly of the fur trade fabulously rich. Frontenac saw no reason why he should not share in the glory of New France—as well as in the colony's wealth.

La Salle had plans of his own. He had seen the richness of the Ohio valley and the fertile lands to the south of Canada. The climate was more pleasant than Canada's, the country more suitable for farming and grazing. By 1673 he had become convinced that the Mississippi River emptied into not the Pacific Ocean but the Gulf of Mexico; the later expeditions of Louis Jolliet and the brave Father Jacques Marquette made him even more certain that this was so.

A fort at the mouth of the Mississippi, he reasoned, would give France control of the heartland of the North American continent, since no foreign ships could then enter or leave the river without French permission. Spain and England—France's chief rivals—would be checkmated. If only he could achieve his goal, the furs, the buffalo skins, the agricultural goods—the entire trade of the continent—would be securely in French hands. But first his base of operations in Canada had to be strong.

Frontenac and La Salle had somewhat different, but related,

& Company with Algonquins meet

Mohawk Oneida Onondaga Cayuga Seneca & Huron

Founding Fort Frontenac at Cataraqui, July, 1673

Louis Henri Buade, Comte de Palluau et de Frontenac

Onontio 👤〜👤 **Torontes'hati**

goals. They saw that by working together they could help each other. Each man respected the other's strengths. Soon they, became allies and close friends.

In 1673, with La Salle's advice, Frontenac moved to put his plan into action. He ordered the towns of Quebec, Montreal, and Three Rivers to supply him with troops and supplies for an expedition into Indian country. It was necessary, he said, to impress the Indians with French military power and also to win their friendship. La Salle was sent to invite the Indians to a conference at Cataraqui, which today is the site of Kingston, Ontario.

On July 12, 1673, Frontenac arrived by water, the one hundred and twenty canoes in his fleet carefully arranged in battle formation. The next day, with great pomp and dignity, the French governor marched his entire force of about four hundred men in their finest dress uniforms before the awe-struck Indians. There were parades, military music, and lavish gifts for the Indians—guns for the men, prunes and raisins for the Indian women and children.

Finally Frontenac and his officers sat around the council fire and smoked peace pipes with the Iroquois chieftains. As governor of New France, Frontenac spoke to the natives in the tone of a stern but protecting father, praising them and promising them the friendship of France. Still, he made clear that his kindness would last only as long as they obeyed him. An imposing figure, always decisive and certain of himself, he was able to win the Indians' respect. The leaders of the five nations—Mohawks, Oneidas, Onondagas, Cayugas, and Senecas—saw him as a man of strength whose words of peace were backed by military might.

A rubbing of the brass plaque commemorating
"Founding Fort Frontenac at Cataraqui, July, 1673"
located in the entrance of the Kingston City Hall

Two flatboats of the French flotilla lay in the river nearby, mounted with cannon.

Even as Frontenac spoke to the chiefs of friendship, his men were busily cutting down trees and digging trenches for the fortress that he and La Salle had planned to build at Cataraqui. The Indians were amazed to see wooden palisades rise, forming the outlines of the fort, in only a few days. But they did nothing to stop the construction.

On July 17 Frontenac called together the Indian chiefs in a council meeting. He set the stage with great formality, lining up his troops in precise formation. Then solemnly he spoke, addressing the Iroquois not as "brothers," the way Frenchmen always had before, but as "children." He offered them friendship, trade, and peace, but threatened to punish them severely for any misdeeds against the French. They should obey only men of character, he said, men like Sieur de La Salle.

By the time Frontenac had returned safely to Quebec, the fort was a reality, commanding Lake Ontario and seriously threatening the trade of the Indians with the English. As Frontenac proudly wrote, he had succeeded in impressing the Iroquois "at once with respect, fear, and good-will."

Not everyone in the French community at Quebec was pleased with Frontenac's success. Some thought that he was acting more out of greed for personal profit than in the interest of France. There were even cries that the fort should be destroyed.

To strengthen his position, Frontenac sent La Salle on a mission to Paris in the autumn of 1674. La Salle carried to Colbert, the minister of finance, who was in charge of Canadian affairs, a letter of recommendation from Governor Frontenac. It described the young explorer as "a man of intelligence and ability, more capable than anybody else I know here to accomplish every kind of enterprise and discovery which may be entrusted to him, as he has the most perfect knowledge of the state of the country."

*Above, an engraving by
J. Grasset St. Sauveur of
an Iroquois warrior.
Below, a map of Fort
Frontenac, drawn about 1685.*

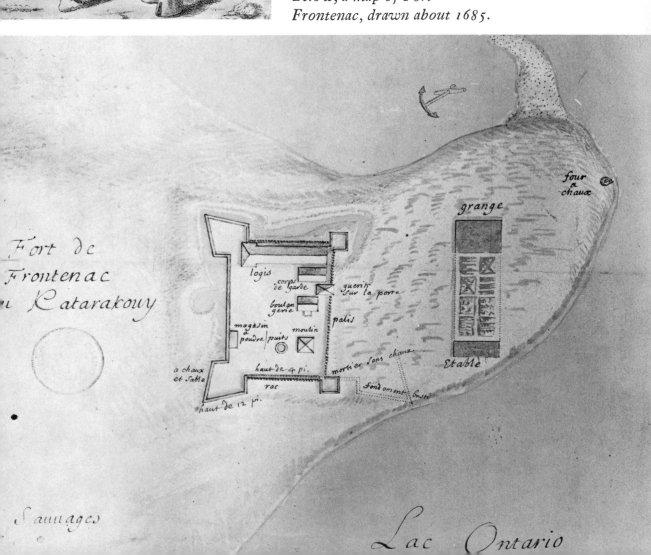

Fort de
Frontenac
u Katarakouy

four
a
chaux

grange

logis
corps
de garde
boulan
gerie
guerit
sur la porte
magasin
a
poudre
puits
moulin
palis

a chaux
et sable
haut de 4 pi.
rac
mortier sans chaux
fondement bastj
Etable

haut de 12 pi.

Sauuages

Lac Ontario

By this time La Salle was known as a loyal supporter and friend of Frontenac.

The reward for his friendship was considerable. During his stay in Paris the king granted his request for admission to the French nobility. He also received a seigneury—authority to govern—at Cataraqui (or, as he had renamed the new outpost, "Fort Frontenac") and exclusive trading rights for the surrounding lands. In return, La Salle promised to pay back the money it had cost to build the fort; he was to maintain it and staff it with soldiers and laborers at his own expense; he was to attract French settlers to the area around the fort; he was to build a church there as soon as possible and support a priest for the community.

Overnight the grant made La Salle one of the most powerful men in Canada. The location of his seigneury gave him a virtual monopoly of the fur trade with the Indians. If he would be content with the privileges of a merchant and "lord of the manor," his fortune was assured for life.

Governor Frontenac and two other men joined in partnership with La Salle in carrying on trade from the outpost. They were bitterly opposed by a group of rival merchants jealous of the monopoly, and by the Jesuits. The Jesuits feared that the expansion of La Salle's control to the western lands would threaten the strength of their foreign missions. Organized fur trading, new settlements, and armed fortifications such as La Salle planned could doom their ambitions for trade and religious conversions in the open territories.

A great struggle began to develop between the small group including La Salle and Frontenac on the one hand and the outraged traders and Jesuit leaders who opposed them. The prize to the winners could be control of New France as well as other enormous portions of the North American continent.

LA SALLE'S
GRAND ENTERPRISE

For three years beginning in 1675, La Salle was totally absorbed in the development of Fort Frontenac and its trading possibilities. He substituted stone ramparts for the original wooden ones and, at his own expense, built a forge, a mill, a bakery, and barracks for the soldiers. As he had promised, he brought Iroquois Indians and French families to settle close to the fort. He arranged for more than one hundred acres of land to be cleared and planted; farm animals were imported from Montreal. To expand the fur trade, he had four ships built to sail Lake Ontario. Nearly two hundred miles removed from Montreal, he reigned almost without supervision as lord of his own little empire.

The jealousy of his enemies, however, flared into vicious plotting. Once there was an attempt to trap him into making love with another man's wife; but La Salle showed no interest in the woman. At another time the Jesuits tried to stir up the Iroquois against him; but Frontenac calmed the Indians, convincing them that the French did not want war. Finally, there was an attempt on La Salle's life. One of his workers, nicknamed Jolycoeur, tried to serve him a salad poisoned with hemlock. But La Salle was only made ill by the poison. When he recovered, he pardoned the guilty man and, despite his suspicions that the Jesuits were involved, refused to blame them in any way.

By the autumn of 1677 La Salle felt ready to take the next step in his grand design for North America. Once again he set out for France. This time, with Frontenac's full support, he asked for permission to establish two new forts and the authority to govern and colonize all the new lands he would explore during the next twenty years. These, he thought, would include all the lands bordering the Mississippi River, and even farther, leading perhaps all the way to Mexico.

King Louis XIV welcomed La Salle's interest in finding a way to Mexico and in exploring the west. The king also granted him the right to build as many fortresses as he considered necessary, as well as a monopoly of the trade in buffalo hides. There were limiting conditions, however. La Salle was not to interfere with the fur trade between the Indians and Montreal; and, more importantly, the entire enterprise was to be completed in five years. Louis XIV hoped to encourage exploration, particularly if it would give France an advantage over Spain and England. But he was opposed to starting new colonies that would spread Canada's small number of French settlers too thinly across the continent. They would be too weak to defend themselves against a strong attack; and, although the king did not say so, they would also be more difficult for him to control.

La Salle accepted the king's conditions and immediately began raising funds to finance his plans. Some Frenchmen, hopeful of profit, willingly gave him loans. But most of the money came from his family, sometimes at incredibly high rates of interest. One of his cousins loaned him eleven thousand livres at 40 percent interest! When he returned to Canada in 1678, Count Frontenac found a lender who would provide fourteen thousand livres —but only in exchange for a mortgage on Fort Frontenac. Desperate for funds, La Salle agreed.

As he gathered together men and supplies for his expedition, La Salle was assisted by two men: Henry de Tonty and Father Louis Hennepin. Tonty was a firm, resourceful Italian officer who had lost a hand in battle; he became La Salle's second in command and his most loyal follower. The remarkable Father Hennepin was a Franciscan friar. Colorful and adventurous, he was passionately eager for travel and preserved a careful journal of his observations. Unfortunately he was given to brash exaggeration of his own role as an explorer; nor did he hesitate to falsify the actual historical record to flatter himself.

Father Hennepin was one of eighteen men who went ahead to Niagara Falls at La Salle's command to begin construction of a new fort. They arrived in the dead of winter, and in order to dig, they first had to use boiled water to soften the ground. The Seneca Indians were greatly displeased when they saw French workers building a fort. Only the coming of La Salle prevented possible violence. He presented the Indians with gifts and soothed their ruffled tempers. His quiet diplomacy persuaded the Senecas to permit the building of a fortified warehouse just above the strategic mouth of the Niagara River. They also allowed La Salle to begin building a ship there.

Before construction could begin on the ship, La Salle's supply vessel ran aground and was wrecked. The only shipbuilding materials saved were some cables and anchors. The situation was so serious, said Father Hennepin, that "anybody but him [La Salle] would have given up the enterprise." But La Salle did not give up. The men worked with primitive tools to lay the keel of the ship. And although it was mid-February, La Salle set out into the snow with two companions to bring supplies from Fort Frontenac—two hundred and fifty miles through the wilderness.

Two days before the men reached Fort Frontenac they ate

*Above, Henry de Tonty.
Below, the building of the*
Griffon, *from Father
Hennepin's* A New Discovery
of a Vast Country in America.

the last kernel of Indian corn in their bag. Blinded by the reflection of the sun against the snow, hungry, thoroughly exhausted, they finally stumbled through the gates of Fort Frontenac.

Scarcely had La Salle arrived when he came face to face with another disaster. His enemies had spread rumors about him, charging that he was a madman whose wild schemes were certain to fail. Those who had loaned him money were alarmed and tried to collect. They seized his property throughout New France, even claiming the seigneury at Fort Frontenac. A long and bitter legal fight began. But La Salle had no patience for that. After putting the matter into the hands of lawyers, he hurried back to Niagara. His mission was more important to him than his personal fortunes.

The ship was ready. It was named the *Griffon* after the monster carved on its bow, copied from Frontenac's coat of arms. Even before La Salle's return, Tonty had launched the ship into the Niagara River. Weighing forty-five tons and equipped with five cannon, it became an object of fear among the Indians, who never before had seen such a large, powerful vessel. They regarded it as a "floating fortress," which of course is exactly what La Salle intended it to be.

In August, 1679, La Salle and his men sailed into Lake Erie aboard the *Griffon*. They made their way to Fort Michilimackinac, the center of Jesuit missionary activity in the Great Lakes area and an important trading post. From there they continued on to Green Bay, trading along the way. On September 18, 1679, La Salle dispatched the *Griffon,* manned by several of his soldiers, back to Fort Frontenac, the hold of the ship crammed with precious furs. They were to use the proceeds from the valuable cargo to pay whatever debts he owed and then return to their starting point, Green Bay. The guns of the *Griffon* thundered a farewell salvo and, with storm clouds gathering on the horizon, the ship sailed away.

It was never seen again. To this day its fate is unknown.

BLOOD, TOIL,
TEARS, AND SWEAT

After the departure of the *Griffon*, La Salle, with fourteen men and four canoes, continued southward to explore the shoreline of Lake Michigan. Meanwhile he had sent Tonty from Michilimackinac with twenty men to collect more furs. The two parties were to meet at the mouth of the Saint Joseph River.

Nothing went right for La Salle's group. First they were driven into rocks by fierce winds, then threatened by hostile Indians. Without food, they were reduced to frightening away buzzards to eat the mangled remains of a deer killed by wolves. Finally the unhappy party reached the point where they were to have met Tonty. But by mid-November he still had not arrived. Many of the men wanted to leave before the winter snows closed in. La Salle refused.

It was almost December before Tonty and his men appeared; they were close to starvation. The *Griffon*, reported Tonty, had never arrived at Michilimackinac.

Hoping to spend the winter with the Illinois Indians, La Salle and his followers, in eight canoes, began to paddle down the Saint Joseph River. Three times La Salle narrowly escaped death. Once he became separated from the expedition while hunting for an Indian trail; after a night alone in the forest, it was only by good fortune that he found his companions. Another time a fire, lighted against the cold in a wigwam he shared with Father Hennepin, ignited the reed mats on which the two men were sleeping; but both escaped.

The morning after the fire, as the party marched along a path, one of the Frenchmen, Duplessis, harboring a grudge, raised his rifle and aimed it at La Salle's back; at the very last minute another soldier deflected the rifle to the side and saved the intrepid leader's life. La Salle chose not even to punish Duplessis.

Shortly after New Year's Day, 1680, La Salle and his men arrived at an encampment of Illinois Indians, near the present city of Peoria. The Indians entertained their visitors by rubbing the feet of the Frenchmen with bear grease and, with their own fingers, putting food into the mouths of the Europeans, as if feeding babies. La Salle provided generous gifts of hatchets and knives.

One night, while the French explorers slept, an Indian chief named Monso, probably in the pay of La Salle's enemies, visited the Illinois chieftains. Monso said that La Salle was really a spy for the Iroquois, and that his true purpose was to stir up tribes beyond the Mississippi to join the Iroquois in a war of total extermination against the Illinois.

La Salle learned of Monso's visit from a friendly Indian on the council of the Illinois. He was not surprised when, at dinner the next night, the brother of the head chief began to tell the Frenchmen outlandish stories about the horrors ahead of them on the Mississippi. According to the Indians, the river was filled with fearsome monsters who would devour them and powerful whirlpools that would pull them to certain death.

Six of La Salle's men, believing the stories, deserted. Then there was another attempt to poison the French adventurer's food; this time he lived only because he carried a special antidote with him.

Just when his situation looked impossible, La Salle befriended a half-starved Illinois warrior, who was returning home after a long hunting trip along the Mississippi. In gratitude the Indian gave him exact details of the landscape along the river. With his new information La Salle was able to meet with the chiefs and accuse them of lying to him about the Mississippi. He described the river so perfectly that the Indians thought he possessed magical powers. La Salle claimed that his knowledge came from "the Master of Life," who had spoken to him. The Indians were astonished. They confessed to lying and asked La Salle to stay among them.

But the bold explorer was eager to take the next step in his plan. Close to the Indian camp on the Illinois River (Lake Peoria) he had been constructing a fortress, which he called Fort Crèvecoeur (Fort Heartbreak). He hoped to build a ship there. Although two of the deserters had been his carpenters, he decided to start the ship anyway. He designed it himself and even began sawing his own planks. After standing by, watching him work, the other men became enthusiastic for the project, too. In less than six weeks the hull was finished.

La Salle now felt able to leave the work of construction at Fort Crèvecoeur in the hands of Tonty and return to Fort Frontenac for anchors and rigging. On March 1, 1680, he set out in the company of four Frenchmen and a Mohegan guide. Separating him from his destination were a thousand miles of territory. There would be snow-covered prairies, forests, icy lakes, and hostile Indians. But without the equipment for his new ship, the whole Mississippi expedition might fail. His plan could be lost.

The trip, as La Salle later described it, was agonizing. He and his men marched by day and slept on the open ground at night; they pushed through bramble thickets and climbed rocks covered with ice and snow; sometimes for whole days they waded through marshland, the water waist-deep or even higher. As the weather grew warmer, rain fell on them in sheets. Toward the end of the journey only La Salle and one other man were not desperately ill.

The news that greeted La Salle at Fort Niagara was calamitous. The *Griffon* had never appeared. Moreover, a ship from France carrying important goods and new recruits for the expedition had been wrecked on the Saint Lawrence River; La Salle's enemies had convinced most of the recruits that he was dead, so that all but a few of the men had returned to France.

Still La Salle continued on. Finally, he and his tiny party emerged from the wilderness at Fort Frontenac, capping a journey of sixty-five days across one third of the continent. They had completed one of the most difficult treks ever made by Frenchmen in North America, overcoming great perils to reach their goal.

At Fort Frontenac the news was even worse. La Salle's creditors, thinking him dead, had seized his property. His own lawyers had cheated him.

Disheartened, but not beaten, La Salle traveled to Montreal. In less than a week he had borrowed enough money to buy all the supplies he needed for Fort Crèvecoeur.

But before he could depart for the west, messengers from Tonty brought word of another crushing blow. Most of the men at Fort Crèvecoeur had rebelled, destroying the encampment. Soon other messengers brought word that the mutineers had continued on to Michilimackinac, where they had stolen valuable furs belonging to La Salle; then they had looted Fort Niagara. With new recruits to help them, about twenty men were on their way to Fort Frontenac, hoping to kill the great commander himself.

Instead of waiting for their arrival, La Salle went out to meet the rebels. Hiding in ambush along the shores of Lake Ontario, he surprised them. He captured and imprisoned most of the deserters, killing two who resisted.

The victory over the mutineers could not, however, bring back Fort Crèvecoeur. Despite all of the risks he had taken, his hard work, his remarkable feats of endurance, there was no question: his plans lay in ruins. Still, La Salle did not give up. On August 10, 1680, he began the thousand-mile journey back to Fort Crèvecoeur. He brought with him a party of twenty-five men, including carpenters, masons, and soldiers, as well as all the supplies he needed to construct a sailing ship to explore the Mississippi River.

THE ROAD
TO GLORY

On returning to the country of the Illinois Indians, La Salle expected to find Tonty and his crew of men hard at work on the ship that would take the French explorers to the mouth of the Mississippi. But what he discovered was very different. At one Indian village after another he recorded scenes of horror. The Iroquois had struck in a ruthless invasion. Sometimes they had waited until the warriors were away, La Salle declared, and then tortured and killed the Illinois women and children; they cooked and ate the flesh of their victims. They destroyed the cornfields, burned the huts. La Salle and his men found pointed stakes in the ground with human skulls stuck on them. Even the graves of dead Indians had been dug up and their bones scattered about. Wolves roamed freely among the corpses. Buzzards feasted.

On the heights of a great cliff where La Salle had ordered Tonty to build a fortress, there was no sign of human life. Heaps of ashes and charred tent poles marked the path of desolation left by the Iroquois. But where was Tonty? And where was Father Hennepin, who, at La Salle's command, had gone to explore and collect furs along the upper Mississippi?

As he expected, Fort Crèvecoeur was completely destroyed. There was no sign of the French garrison. On one plank of the ship's hull, which surprisingly remained intact, was scrawled the message *"Nous sommes tous sauvages"* ("We are all savages").

RENE-ROBERT DE LA SALLE

EXPLORATION
1673-1687

Arkansas R.

Brazos R.

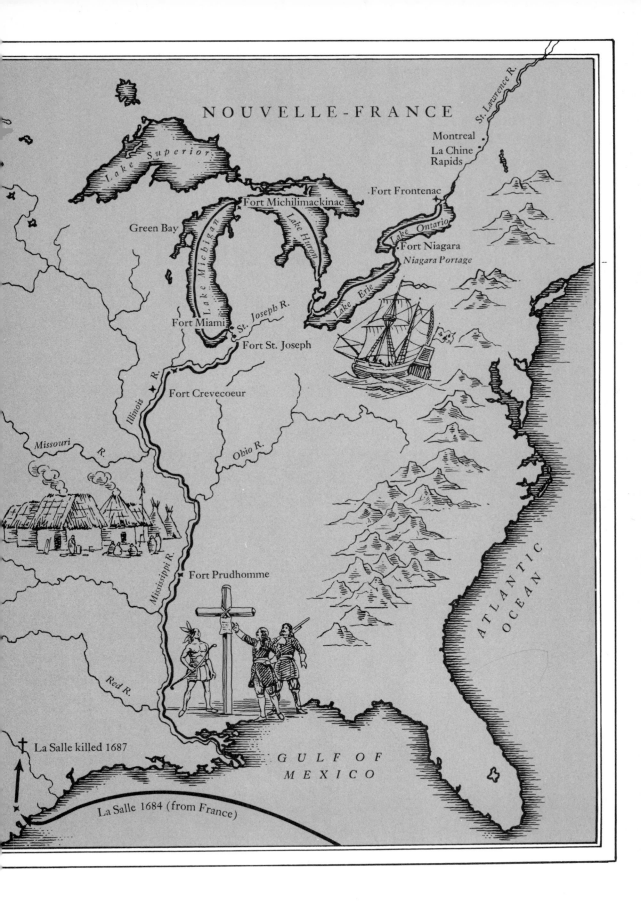

NOUVELLE-FRANCE

Lake Superior

Montreal
La Chine
Rapids

St. Lawrence R.

Fort Michilimackinac

Fort Frontenac

Green Bay

Lake Michigan

Lake Huron

Lake Ontario

Fort Niagara

Niagara Portage

Fort Miami

St. Joseph R.

Fort St. Joseph

Lake Erie

Illinois R.

Fort Crevecoeur

Missouri R.

Ohio R.

Mississippi R.

Fort Prudhomme

Red R.

ATLANTIC OCEAN

La Salle killed 1687

GULF OF MEXICO

La Salle 1684 (from France)

Clearly, the phrase was the handiwork of the same murderous Frenchmen who had deserted and joined in the pillage.

La Salle searched in vain for his lost comrades. Then, with cold weather coming on, he set up a temporary headquarters at Fort Miami, on the Saint Joseph River, near Lake Michigan. There he spent the winter of 1680–81.

Under the vastly different circumstances in which he found himself, La Salle began to change his plan. He now thought it might be best to join together the Indian tribes of the west in a great league against the Iroquois. It would be possible, he thought, to organize a colony of Indians and have Franciscan friars teach them the arts of civilization. The Indians, reasoned La Salle, could buy French goods in exchange for the valuable furs of the area. Meanwhile, he could gather strong forces for his conquest of the Mississippi.

During 1681 many Indians agreed to become the allies of the French. The Shawnees joined La Salle. So did some Abnakis and Mohegans who had fled from New England following their defeat in King Philip's War. La Salle was a master orator, even in the Indian languages, and after one of his great speeches the Miamis were persuaded to follow him.

In early March La Salle set out to obtain supplies for the Illinois, who were hoping to return to their devastated homes. But traveling in the open prairie, with the brilliant sun reflecting off

Below, engraving of Indians plundering Father Hennepin's party in 1680, from his book Voyage Curieux, *published in 1704. Center, title page of an English edition of Father Hennepin's* A New Discovery of a Vast Country in America, *published in 1699. Top, signature of Count de Frontenac on a document of land transfer, October 15, 1681.*

A New Diſcovery of a Large Country in AMERICA by Father Lewis Hennepin

A
New Diſcovery
OF A
Vaſt Country in *America*,
Extending above Four Thouſand Miles,
BETWEEN
New France & *New Mexico*;
WITH A
Deſcription of the Great *Lakes*, *Cataraĉts*,
Rivers, *Plants*, and *Animals*.
Alſo, the *Manners*, *Cuſtoms*, and *Languages* of the ſeveral
Native *Indians*; And the Advantage of Commerce with
thoſe different Nations.

WITH A
CONTINUATION
Giving an ACCOUNT of the
Attempts of the Sieur *de la SALLE* upon the
Mines of St. *Barbe*, &c. The Taking of *Quebec*
by the *Engliſh*; With the Advantages of a
ſhorter Cut to *China* and *Japan*.

Both Illuſtrated with *Maps*, and *Figures*; and Dedicated
to His Majeſty King *WILLIAM*.

By *L. Hennepin* now Reſident in *Holland*.

To which are added, Several *New Diſcoveries* in *North-America*, not Publiſh'd in the *French* Edition.

the snow, he and several of his men fell victim to snow blindness. It was several days before they recovered.

Outagamie warriors who befriended La Salle during his illness gave him good news. Tonty had been seen alive. As soon as he was well enough to travel, La Salle set out for Michilimackinac, hoping for further word of Tonty. To his delight, he found the steadfast Italian explorer there—in perfect health and overjoyed at their reunion. Even the usually cold, reserved La Salle was deeply moved to see his comrade again. Father Hennepin had meanwhile returned to France to claim credit for his own explorations and for some that had been undertaken by La Salle alone.

Scarcely losing a day's time after their meeting, La Salle and Tonty took to their canoes. Together they made the one-thousand-mile journey back to Montreal. There they pleaded for more money to carry out their major task—the voyage down the Mississippi. For now, the Illinois colony would have to wait.

With the support of Count Frontenac they managed to borrow enough money to buy supplies. They also hired a force of twenty-two Frenchmen and a motley crew of some thirty Indians, including ten squaws and three Indian children, since the men refused to leave their families behind.

There were angry accusations that La Salle's "insane scheme" had already cost too much property and the lives of too many young men; but the passionate French leader insisted on continuing. Since he was a man of iron will, discipline, and determination, there could be no outcome for him but victory or death.

It was nearly Christmas Day, 1681, before La Salle and his party ended an exhausting overland march and began to descend the Illinois River. La Salle had given up his plan of constructing a large ship for his purposes. Instead, he placed himself at the head of a formation of frail but fast-moving canoes. On February 13,

1682, he launched his little fleet into the powerful current of the Mississippi. The caravan was carried along swiftly past the mouth of the Missouri. Farther downstream the rolling tide of the river was swelled by the broad, slow-moving waters of the Ohio.

At first the party of explorers stopped only to hunt the wild turkeys, swans, deer, and buffalo that were abundant along the riverbanks. Then when one of the group, Pierre Prudhomme, wandered away and was lost, they stopped to build a stockade while rescue parties searched for him. Ten days later Prudhomme, near starvation, floated down the river on a log. La Salle left him with a small force to man the stockade, named in his honor Fort Prudhomme, and pressed on.

The Indian tribes they met were generally friendly. One tribe, the Arkansas, feasted and entertained the strangers for three days. La Salle wrote later of his admiration for their tall, beautifully formed bodies, their honesty (nothing belonging to the French was stolen), and their good nature. Two Arkansas tribesmen even volunteered to accompany La Salle as guides to the lower reaches of the river.

About one hundred miles beyond the mouth of the Arkansas River they encountered another tribe, the Taensas. These Indians lived in large huts built from sun-baked mud and covered by domed roofs. They worshiped the sun, sacrificing victims to that god before a sacred fire in a domed temple. Their dignified chief considered himself a living descendant of the sun god. La Salle and Tonty gave the chief generous gifts and were again well treated by the Indians.

At the villages of the Natchez and the Koroas Indians, too, they met with warm welcomes. At each village La Salle planted a large cross and raised the flag of Louis XIV. A priest, Father Membré, led the singing of hymns, and three salvos of shots were fired from the explorers' muskets. Always La Salle claimed the

Below, manuscript copy of a La Salle map by William Kingsford, showing "the Sources of the Mississippi." Above, an old print contrasting the summer and winter costumes of the Indians in Louisiana

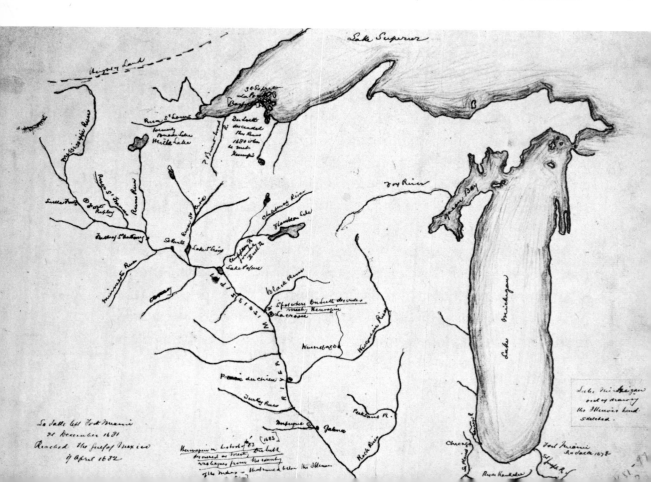

new territories in the name of the king of France, formally taking possession of the new lands. The Indians whose lands he was claiming usually stood by, not understanding the meaning of the strange ceremony that was intended to deprive them of their homeland. Only one tribe, the Quinipissas, attacked the Frenchmen; La Salle stopped just long enough to frighten them away.

On April 6, 1682, the French explorers came upon the delta of the Mississippi, at the present site of New Orleans. Here the river divided into three channels, all marked by the smell of seawater. La Salle was near his goal.

On April 9 he reached the Gulf of Mexico. With great rejoicing among the Frenchmen, he planted a cross. At its base he buried deep in the ground a copper plate with the coat of arms of France. Alongside the cross he raised a column, also with the French coat of arms. Then in a simple speech he took possession of the entire Mississippi River valley, which he called "Louisiana" in honor of the king. Next there were solemn hymns led by the priests. Finally the soldiers exploded with shouts of *"Vive le roi!"* —"Long live the king!" They fired salvos of shots into the air and cheered the accomplishment of their great leader, La Salle.

On that spring day in 1682 alongside the Mississippi, René-Robert Cavelier, Sieur de La Salle, laid claim to an incredible domain extending from the Allegheny Mountains on the east to the Rocky Mountains on the west; from the Great Lakes on the north to the Rio Grande River and the Gulf of Mexico on the south. It was an area of boundless wealth in farmland and mineral resources. With a few words uttered in a simple ceremony before some puzzled Indians and a few of his countrymen, La Salle had given France title to a mighty empire. He had also entered his name forever in the history of discovery and exploration. Not since Christopher Columbus's discovery of America had any one man made such a tremendous claim of territory.

LAST VOYAGES

It was one thing to lay claim to an empire, quite another thing to govern it. La Salle was determined to see his dream of empire come true, but there were many obstacles in the way.

The return trip up the river was a nightmare. At first there was little food but alligator meat. The Quinipissas buzzed angrily at the Frenchmen's heels, harassing them with arrows. Then La Salle, despite his iron will and strong body, fell desperately ill. For forty days, as he later wrote, he lay at Fort Prudhomme, his very life hanging in the balance. For four months afterward he remained badly weakened. Because of his illness he was unable to leave for France to report his discoveries to the king and win support for the construction of a city at the mouth of the Mississippi.

Instead, he ordered Tonty to begin building a fort at "Starved Rock"—a steep cliff some 125 feet above the Illinois River, just south of Lake Michigan. There he hoped to set up a strong defense point against the Iroquois and also to store the furs collected in trade with the western tribes. He named his lofty eagle's nest Fort Saint Louis. Almost overnight he miraculously persuaded some four thousand Indian warriors and their families to join the small core of French settlers living there under his protection.

Suddenly, because of political intrigue in Europe, the situation changed completely. The enemies of La Salle and Frontenac convinced authorities in France to replace Count Frontenac as governor. His successor was Le Febvre de la Barre—a weak, greedy old man nominated by the Jesuits; he was determined to destroy La Salle's plans and take his property.

La Barre wrote to Louis XIV, accusing La Salle of trying to set up an empire of his own in the west; of endangering New France by arousing the Iroquois to war; and of trading in beaver skins with the Indians near Montreal, which the king's original patent had strictly forbidden him to do. Only this last charge against him was true.

Acting quickly, La Barre seized Fort Frontenac. He refused to send ammunition and supplies to Fort Saint Louis, and then seized it, too. Secretly he urged the Iroquois to find La Salle and kill him.

In the early autumn of 1683 La Salle managed to reach Quebec. From there he eluded La Barre and sailed for France to plead his cause.

At the court of Louis XIV, the dignified, persuasive La Salle was received as a hero. His exploits in the wilderness of North America were the talk of Paris. He wrote about his adventures and gave extensive interviews.

It was the right time to visit. The king, fighting an undeclared war with Spain, leaped at the prospect of establishing a base on the Gulf of Mexico to strike at his enemies. He ordered La Salle to return to the New World. There the explorer was to set up a fort and secure the lower Mississippi. He was then to prepare for an attack across Texas on the Spanish colony of Mexico.

Louis granted La Salle a fleet of four ships, including the *Joly*, a vessel of thirty-six guns with a crew of seventy. Also numbered in his force were one hundred soldiers, thirty civilian volunteers (among them a few gentlemen of rank), and even some families and unmarried girls to help establish French colonies. Several missionaries agreed to accompany the expedition; one of them was La Salle's own brother, the Abbé Jean Cavelier. La Salle was to be governor of any territories he conquered in Louisiana, as well as of the entire Illinois territory.

Meanwhile, King Louis himself wrote to La Barre, demanding in anger that he return Fort Frontenac and Fort Saint Louis to La Salle, along with any other property of the explorer that he had seized.

On July 24, 1684, the expedition set sail for the New World. From the beginning there was trouble. Sieur de Beaujeu, a captain in the French navy, was put in charge of the ships. La Salle never enjoyed sharing his authority with anyone; he also suspected Beaujeu of being sympathetic to his enemies, the Jesuits. Beaujeu in turn considered La Salle too secretive about his plans and, lacking a full title of nobility, fit to command only Indians and frontiersmen—certainly not regular French soldiers. Besides, wrote Beaujeu: "There are very few people who do not think that his brain is touched."

After two months at sea, the ships struggled toward port at Santo Domingo, the three smaller craft lagging behind the *Joly*. Many of the passengers had become ill during the voyage. La Salle was one of them, the victim of a serious fever that kept him delirious for many days. While he recovered, one of the ships still out at sea, the *St. Francis*, was separated from the others and captured by Spanish pirates. Aboard the *St. Francis* were valuable tools and supplies that could not be replaced; furthermore, its

A transcription of an account of Robert de La Salle's last expedition, written by his brother Jean, around 1690

Monseigneur

Voicy la Relation du voyage
que mon Frere entreprit pour
decouvrir dans le golfe du mexique
lembouchure du Fleuve de mississipy
Une mort inopinée et tragique layant
empeché delaparachever et d'en
rendre Conte a vôtre grandeur,
Jespere quelle Agreera que Je suplée
a son defaut

Le mois de Juillet 1684 nous sortis
mes delarochelle au nombre de
quatre voilles avec on fort beautemps
lasaison semblort nous prometre la
Continuation et ne devoit vray
semblablement nous faire Craindre
que le Calme ou les grandes
Chaleurs neanmoingts lafin du mois
nous donna vnetourmente qui des
mots lenavire que montoit mon
Frere et nous Contreguit tous a
rétachir dansleport d'ou nous
estions partis, nous remis mes
ala voille et peu de Jours aprés
vnefeconde tourmente disperssau
nostre petite flote; le st Francois
Fust Pris par des chalupes es-
pagnolles, etles trois autres ne
se Refoignirent quau petit goave

crew revealed to Spanish authorities La Salle's plan for colonizing Louisiana.

By the end of November, 1684, La Salle was well enough to travel. He led his three remaining ships into the Gulf of Mexico— a sea forbidden to all white men but Spaniards by a decree of Philip II of Spain in the previous century. Before, when La Salle had canoed down from Canada to the mouth of the Mississippi, he had been unable to chart the river's exact longitude. Nor were the pilots of his ships familiar with the gulf; they exaggerated the strength of currents flowing eastward. As a result the little French expedition landed far to the west of the river's entrance, probably near the site of today's Corpus Christi, Texas.

Shortly afterward, La Salle's supply ship, the *Aimable*, ran aground on a sandbar and was destroyed. It was a serious blow. According to the journal of Joutel, the commander's loyal aide, the captain of the ship wrecked it intentionally out of dislike for La Salle by disobeying signals to stay out to sea. Some of the men complained, rightly, that no landing should have been made before the Mississippi was found.

La Salle, admitting now that he was lost, decided to construct a rough fortification and at least start to form a colony. But the unhappy company's misfortunes grew. The food and water were unsanitary. Disease spread quickly. Every day four or five persons died. The Indians howled through the night, stole blankets and other articles, and set fires around the camp. Most of the colonists'

Above, an engraving depicting the many problems for La Salle, from Hennepin's Nouveau Voyage, *published in 1698. Below, the camp of La Salle near Matagorda Bay, from* The Romance *by A. L. Mason, published in 1883.*

livestock died. Attempts to raise food by farming generally failed. Deadly rattlesnakes terrorized the settlers.

To make matters worse, the *Joly*, sent in the direction of Mobile Bay for supplies, embarked instead for France. Beaujeu, pitiless, never returned with aid for the expedition. Not long afterward La Salle's fourth and last ship, the *Belle*, was wrecked with the loss of most of its crew. Only 40 of the original 185 colonists remained alive. Without ships there was only one way that they could ever hope to return to their homeland—they had to find the Mississippi River and make their way northward to Canada.

La Salle and a scouting party of twenty men set out in search of what they now called "the fatal river." Only eight of the men returned to the fort; some deserted to live a life of savagery, others were simply lost, and one was eaten by an alligator. Among the explorers who did return were La Salle's brother, the Abbé Cavelier, and his nephew, Moranget.

In January, 1687, leaving about twenty settlers behind, including the surviving women and children, La Salle and the remainder of the once proud expedition set out for Canada to obtain aid. The scene of their lingering farewell was one of deep sadness; those who left and those who stayed behind knew they might never see each other again.

For more than two months La Salle and his men marched north and eastward. Then, one day in the middle of March, there was a fatal quarrel. Moranget, La Salle's nephew, grew angry when some of the men sent out to hunt reserved the best meat for themselves. Old grudges leaped to the surface.

A map of the vicinity of La Salle's camp on Matagorda Bay, taken to France by Captain de Beaujeu

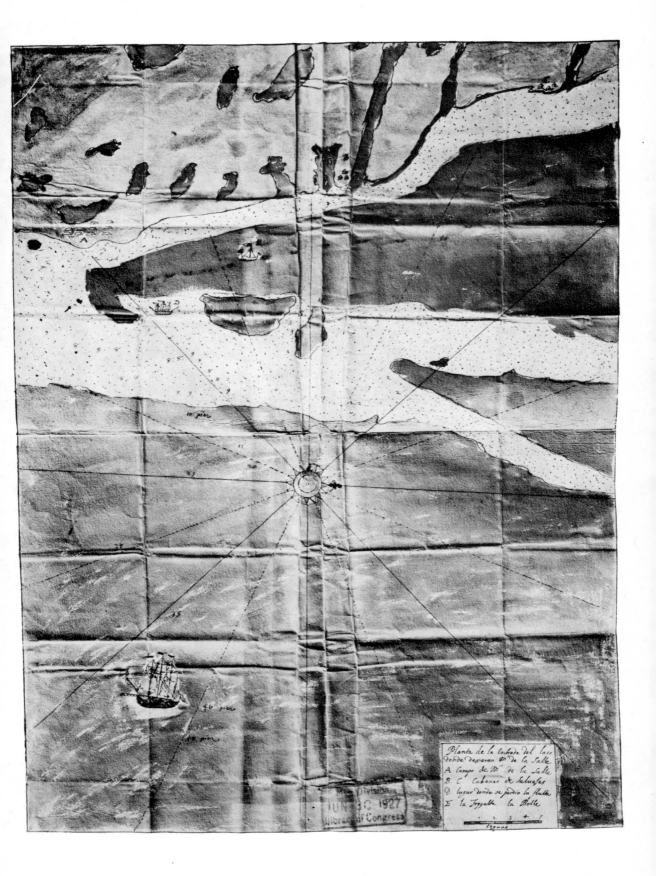

Planta de la Entrada del lago
donde desparon Mr de la Salle
A. Campo de Mr de la Salle
B. C. Cabanas de Saluajes
D. lugar donde se perdio la Flutte
E. la Fregatte la Belle

The surgeon, Liotot, and two other conspirators agreed to take revenge. They waited until Moranget, La Salle's loyal Indian hunter Nika, and a servant were asleep. Then, with an ax, Liotot killed all three men.

Having done the bloody deed, the mutineers decided there would be no way to hide from La Salle the murder of his nephew. He would not allow them to return to civilization. Therefore he, too, would have to die.

Alarmed when the hunting party failed to return, La Salle came to look for the men. L'Archevêque, one of the killers, greeted his commander with taunting insults to distract him. Meanwhile, Liotot and the third conspirator, Duhaut, waited in ambush. When La Salle came near, they both fired their pistols. Shot through the head, the great leader died instantly. René-Robert Cavelier, Sieur de La Salle, at the age of forty-three, was no more. The killers stripped his body of clothing and valuables and then left it unburied for the wolves and buzzards to devour.

Eventually, one of the murderers fled to live with the Indians; Duhaut and Liotot were both shot to death by one of the surviving Frenchmen. The other survivors, including La Salle's brother Abbé Cavelier and the faithful Joutel—whose diary tells the story of the ill-fated expedition—made their way to Quebec and from there home to France.

King Louis refused to send a relief force to rescue the settlers left behind at the makeshift fort in Texas. Spanish soldiers who visited the site of the fort in late April, 1689, discovered a scene of death and desolation. They learned from French deserters living among the Indians that about three months earlier the colony

Death of La Salle, from the English
edition of Father Hennepin's A New
Discovery of a Vast Country in America

51

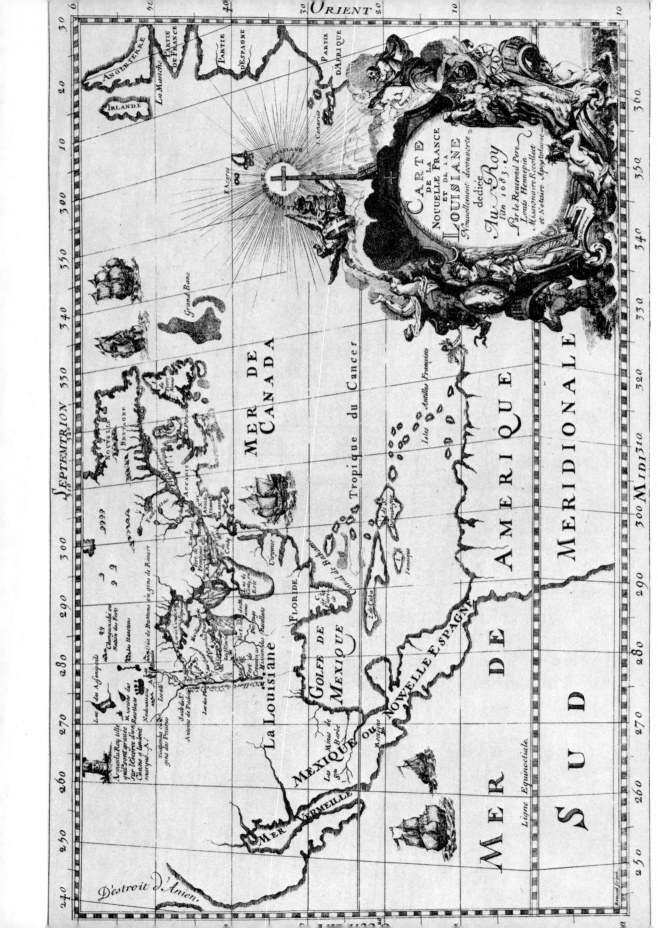

ORIENT

SEPTEMTRION

MIDI

ANGLETERRE

IRLANDE

La Manche

PARTIE DE FRANCE

PARTIE D'ESPAGNE

I. Canarie

PARTIE D'ARRIQUE

I. Acores

Grand Banc

MER DE CANADA

NOUELLE BRETAGNE

ACCADIE

Tropique du Cancer

Isles Antilles Françaises

FLORIDE

GOLFE DE MEXIQUE

Canal de Bahama

I. de Cuba

Jamaique

La Louisiane

MEXIQUE ou NOUELLE ESPAGNE

MER VERMEILLE

MER DE AMERIQUE MERIDIONALE

Ligne Equinoctiale.

MER DE SUD

Destroit d'Anien.

CARTE DE LA NOUUELLE FRANCE ET DE LA LOUISIANE Nouuellement decouuerte dediée Au Roy l'an 1683. Par le Reuerend Pere Louis Hennepin. Missionaire Recollet et Notaire Apostolique.

had ceased to exist. Almost all of the settlers had perished from disease or at the hands of Indian raiders; the fate of a few children rescued by Indian women remains a mystery.

So ended La Salle's dream of founding a great French empire in the heartland of America. He had established forts, organized Indian alliances, traveled where no other white man had ever been before. Yet of all those efforts, little survived. Others had to do the monotonous, painstaking work of planting crops and building cities, tasks for which he had no patience. All that remained of his years of heroism was the example of his energy and unconquerable will.

He had concentrated his entire being toward the achievement of a single ambitious goal. He braved hunger, fatigue, disease, cold, heat, and the jealous plotting of his enemies with patience and courage. No hardship was too great, no suffering too severe as, joylessly, he sacrificed everything else to attain his ends. La Salle trusted nobody but himself, listened to no advice, cared not at all for pleasure or popularity. He prided himself in suppressing his emotions—he had no wife and appeared to care little for the company of women.

A complicated man, driven to succeed regardless of the risk to his own or his men's safety, he inspired either intense loyalty or great hatred. In that sense, like other deeply committed, visionary adventurers of history, he carried within his own personality the seeds of his triumphs and also of his destruction.

A map showing the domain of New France in North America, including Louisiana, made in 1683

A NOTE
ON SOURCES

La Salle's letters and journals have been collected and published, but no complete English translation is available. Portions of his papers and excerpts from accounts by Father Hennepin, Father Membré, Henry de Tonty, Henri Joutel, and Jean Cavelier may be found in translation in Isaac J. Cox, *The Journeys of René-Robert Cavelier, Sieur de La Salle*, 2 volumes, A. S. Barnes (New York, 1905).

By far the most important modern work is the study by the distinguished American historian Francis Parkman, *La Salle and the Discovery of the Great West* (1879), the third volume in his monumental seven-part work, *France and England in North America*, reprinted by Frederick Ungar Publishing Company (New York, 1965). Also important are John Brebner's *The Explorers of North America, 1492–1806* and *With La Salle Down the Mississippi* by David C. G. Libby.

INDEX

Abnaki Indians, 36
Aimable (ship), 47
Algonquin Indians, 12
Allegheny Mountains, 41
Arkansas Indians, 39

Beaujeu, Sieur de, 44, 48
Belle (ship), 48
Bonaparte, Napoleon, 1

California, Gulf of, 6
Canada, 4, 17
Cataraqui, 19, 20, 22
Cayuga Indians, 19
Champlain, Samuel de, 12
China, 1
China Rapids, 4
Columbus, Christopher, 6, 41
Cortes, Hernando, 1
Crèvecoeur, Fort, 30, 31, 32, 33

De Courcelle, Governor, 6, 9
Dollier de Casson, François, 9, 15
Duhaut (assassin), 51
Duquesne, Fort, 15

England, 16, 17, 24

Fort Crèvecoeur, 30, 31, 32, 33
Fort Duquesne, 15

Fort Frontenac, 22, 23, 24, 25, 27, 30, 31, 42–43, 44
    mortgage on, 24
Fort Miami, 36
Fort Michilimackinac, 27, 28, 31, 38
Fort Niagara, 31
Fort Prudhomme, 39, 42
Fort Saint Louis, 42, 43, 44
France, 1, 12, 24, 41
    title to Mississippi River valley, 41
    See also Louis XIV
Frontenac, Count de, 16, 17, 19, 20, 22, 24, 38
    friendship with La Salle, 17–22
    replacement of, as governor, 43
Frontenac, Fort, 22, 23, 24, 25, 27, 30, 31, 42, 43, 44
Fur trade, 17, 22, 24, 36

Great Britain, 16
    See also England
Great Lakes, 2, 41
Green Bay, 27
Griffon (ship), 27, 28, 31
Gulf of California, 6
Gulf of Mexico, 2, 17, 41, 47

Hennepin, Father Louis, 25, 28, 38
Huron Indians, 12

Illinois Indians, 28, 29, 33, 36
Illinois River, 15, 30, 38
Indians, 4, 6, 9, 12, 13, 19, 20
    friendship with La Salle, 13, 16, 19,
      20, 29, 30, 39
Iroquois Indians, 12, 19, 23, 29, 33, 43

Jefferson, Thomas, 1
Jesuits, 3, 9, 22, 23, 27, 43, 44
    hatred of La Salle, 23
Jolliet, Louis, 13, 17
Joly (ship), 43, 44, 48
Joutel, Henri, 47, 51

King Philip's War, 36
Kingston, Ont. *See* Cataraqui; Fort
  Frontenac
Koroas Indians, 39

La Barre, Le Febvre de, 43, 44
La Chine (Saint Sulpice), 4, 9, 12
La Salle, Jean Cavelier de (brother), 4,
  44, 48, 51
La Salle, René-Robert Cavelier de
    achievements of, 2
    aid from Louis XIV, 43–44
    childhood of, 3
    death of, 51
    discovery of Mississippi River val-
      ley, 41
    early explorations, 12–16
    financial aid for explorations, 6–9
    friendship with Frontenac, 17–22
    friendship with Indians, 13, 16, 19,
      20, 29, 30, 39
    last voyages of, 42–53
    love of exploring, 1–2, 6
    mutiny against, 31–32, 51
    religious training, 3–4
Lake Erie, 15, 27
Lake Huron, 9

Lake Michigan, 28, 33
Lake Ontario, 9, 12, 17, 20, 23
Lake Peoria, 30
Lake Superior, 13
L'Archevêque (assassin), 51
Liotot (surgeon), 51
Louis XIV, king of France, 1, 24, 39,
  43, 51
    aid to La Salle, 43–44
Louisiana, 1, 41, 44

Marquette, Father Jacques, 17
Membré, Father, 39
Mexico, 2, 24, 43
Mexico, Gulf of, 2, 17, 41, 47
Miami, Fort, 36
Miami Indians, 36
Michilimackinac, Fort, 27, 28, 31, 38
Mississippi River, 1, 2, 6, 17, 24, 29, 30,
  32, 33, 36, 39, 41, 42, 48
    La Salle's discovery of, 41
Missouri River, 39
Mobile Bay, 48
Mohawk Indians, 19
Monso (Indian chief), 29
Montreal, 4, 15, 16, 19, 23, 31, 38, 43
Moranget (La Salle's nephew), 48,
  49

Natchez Indians, 39
New France, 17, 19, 22, 27, 43
New Orleans, 41
Niagara, Fort, 31
Niagara Falls, 13, 25, 27
Nipising Indians, 9

Ohio River, 2, 6, 13, 15, 17
Oneida Indians, 19
Onondaga Indians, 19
Order of Saint Sulpice, 4
Outagamie Indians, 38

Pacific Ocean, 6, 17
Paris, 20, 22, 43
Parkman, Francis, 15
Peoria, 29
Philip II, king of Spain, 47
Pittsburgh, 1
Pizarro, Francisco, 1
Prudhomme, Fort, 39, 42
Prudhomme, Pierre, 39
Potawatomi Indians, 13

Quebec, 6, 19, 20, 43
Queylus, Abbé de, 6
Quinipissa Indians, 41, 42

Rio Grande River, 41
Rocky Mountains, 41

St. Francis (ship), 44

Saint Joseph River, 28, 33
Saint Lawrence River, 4, 31
Saint Louis, Fort, 42, 43, 44
Saint Sulpice (La Chine), 4, 9, 12
Saint Sulpice, Order of, 4
    See also Sulpicians
Santo Domingo, 44
Seneca Indians, 6, 12, 13, 15, 19,
    25
    friendship with La Salle, 13
Shawnee Indians, 36
Spain, 2, 17, 24, 43, 47
Sulpicians, 4, 9, 12, 13–15

Taensas Indians, 39
Texas, 43, 51
Three Rivers, 19
Tonty, Henry de, 25, 27, 28, 30, 31, 33,
    38, 39, 42

ABOUT THE AUTHOR

William Jay Jacobs has taught at Hunter College and Brooklyn College, as well as at Rutgers and Harvard universities. He is the author of numerous historical works, including *Search for Freedom: America and its People* and a series of twentieth-century biographies. Dr. Jacobs has written the Visual Biographies of *Prince Henry the Navigator, Hernando Cortes, Samuel de Champlain, William Bradford of Plymouth Colony,* and *Roger Williams.*